HELP!

I'M CONFUSED ABOUT CREDIT AND DEBT

Martin Sweet

Consulting Editor: Dr. Jim Winter

First printed 2016

ISBN 978-1-84625-526-7

Published by Day One Publications
Ryelands Road, Leominster, HR6 8NZ
Tel 01568 613 740 Fax 01568 611 473
North America Toll Free 888 329 6630
email—sales@dayone.co.uk
website—www.dayone.co.uk

Printed by Orchard Press Cheltenham Ltd

Contents

Introduction: The Credit Trap

Credit and money are among the toughest areas of life for people to get their heads around today. We live in a society which is continually bombarding us with the latest 'must have' item. Many people, even when times are hard, have quite a sizeable disposable income; others have very little—but the temptation is the same: spend all you have and then some. Marketing companies have researched their target audiences and their adverts are carefully designed to engage and appeal to us. At the same time, banks and building societies have made it all too easy for people to take out loans or get credit cards. Now and again the media and politicians say how dangerous this is, but nothing really changes and lessons are rarely learned where the possibility of making a quick buck is concerned. The mixture of wonderful gadgets and the latest fashions, together with the ability to get the money to buy them, is a powerfully tempting brew. It is not surprising, then, that so many people, young and old, get caught in 'the credit trap'. Conversely, there are many who through no fault of their own find themselves with barely enough to live on, but are still attracted by all that the world has to offer and are sucked into situations they can't afford.

Much of the discussion about credit and debt concentrates on whether or not it is right to get into debt, and we will examine this in the booklet; however, the real issue behind credit and debt is a state of heart and mind.

As with every other problem in life, we need to start out from the right place with the right tools if we are to tackle it properly. I assume that, if you are reading this booklet, it is because you want to get this money thing right. I am also assuming that you want to get living your life right too. For these issues, just as with anything else in life, you need to have God central in your thinking.

Here is an interesting statistic: while there are nearly a thousand references to faith and prayer in the Bible, there are over *seven thousand* references to money and possessions. One in every ten verses in the Gospels deals with these things. This underlines the importance of the subject, and the fact that God has plenty to say about it to help us.

Matthew 6:33 says,

> *But seek first the kingdom of God and His righteousness, and all these things [food, clothing, etc.] shall be added to you.*

In other words, to get things right in our lives we need first to get our relationship with God right. The temptation is to concentrate on sorting out these 'horizontal' problems (that is, everyday problems such as debt, relationships, health worries) using our wisdom and strength, but God turns this upside down in this verse. Of course, all these pressure points in life are important, but God tells us here that they must be secondary to getting right with God: get this 'vertical' relationship (our relationship with God) right and all the others will start to make sense, even if they're not easy to deal with.

Paying our debt

What does it cost you and me to get right with God? Absolutely nothing! How much did it cost God? It cost Him His Son, Jesus Christ. Because we are all sinners, we could never have got ourselves right with God on our own, but that is why Jesus came to earth all those years ago—to die on the cross to pay the price for our sin. You could say that we were in debt, a debt of sin that we could never, ever hope to pay—but Jesus came along and, because He loved us so much, He gave His life to pay that debt for us. Matthew 20:28 puts it like this:

> *The Son of Man did not come to be served, but to serve, and to give His life a ransom for many.*

If you were in a position of having someone pay off a huge debt for you, you would be a fool not to take the gift gratefully. It is just the same with our debt of sin. Jesus offers us the free gift of forgiveness of sins and eternal life. All you have to do is turn away from your sins and trust that Christ died for you to make you right with God. If you have never done this, I urge you to do so now. Salvation is a free gift offered by God; it would be foolish not to accept it. Once you have done this, the 'horizontal' problem of how to deal with money will make a whole lot more sense.

The problem and its solution

The problem: the trap is set

Much of the problem with money is in our heads. It is usually found in how we think about, and our attitude towards, what we have or don't have. This is called our mindset. There are two basic mindsets that cover just about every situation.

Mindset 1

Imagine you are walking past a shop window and your attention is caught by something. 'This thing is just what I want,' you say. 'I want to have it. I must have it! But I can't afford it—I don't have enough money. What am I to do?' Here is where Mindset 1 comes in. I can't afford it, but I want it, and I want it now. I can't wait until I have saved up for it, until I have enough money—that will take months, even years! What can

I do? I must find more money than I currently have, so I'll have to borrow it. I'll find someone to lend me the money, then I'll have enough, and I can buy what I want in just a couple of days or even today! Oh, and I can easily pay back the money sometime later. Don't worry about the details—I can have it now. Yes!

This might sound a bit extreme, and many real-life situations will be less black and white; but ultimately behind this mindset is the belief that something other than God can satisfy us and make us happy.

Mindset 2

Mindset 2 is different. Same scenario, same shop window, same desirable 'something', same lack of money. This time you say: I can't afford it, but I want it. What am I to do? I really would like it now, but I simply don't have the money for it. I will save up and wait until I have enough money to buy it, even if it takes months or years. It will be hard to wait—but when I get it, it will be mine, and I won't have got into debt. If God wants me to have it, then I'll get it in His time, not mine.

There is only one real difference between these two mindsets. Mindset 1 has a problem, one that our society does its best to exploit. Have you ever seen a small child playing contentedly until suddenly he or she sees a new toy? Most often, the child will immediately want the new toy and do his or her level best to get it straight away. If the parent tries to slow this process down for any reason, that will most likely be met by the toddler's full fury: tears, screams, tantrums—we've all seen it. You see, young children have to learn that they can't always have what they want immediately; sometimes they have to be patient and wait. Children aren't born with the ability to wait patiently; they have to learn it the hard way. After a while, most of us grow out of this stage, and as we mature we know we have to go along with the rules and wait—even if on the inside we still want to grab the toy and run!

The problem is that today's culture is trying to un-teach us this! If you don't believe me, just take a look at the adverts on TV. Many try to tell us that we are the centre of the universe—we deserve whatever it is we want, we have a right to it. Others say that we must have it simply because it is the latest must-have. Buy while stocks last. Sale ends today. Still others say we can have it now: 'Buy now, pay nothing until January.' 'First year free.' 'Easy repayments.' Peer pressure doesn't help either: we want to be in with the crowd, to fit in. Your neighbour has got one. Your best mate is showing off his 'must-have' too.

What is the result of all this? That there is more pressure than ever before for everyone to have 'it', whatever the cost; and we are bombarded by a way of thinking that is unwilling to wait. No age group is excluded from this, but I think it is hardest for teenagers, the ones who are most susceptible to these pressures and who have the least experience of life to help them through.

This isn't a new problem; we can even read about it in the Bible. Nearly four thousand years ago there was a young man with a 'must have now' mentality, and his brother was there to exploit it! Esau came in after a hard day's hunting and he was very hungry. His brother Jacob had just made some stew and Esau wanted it: 'Please feed me with that same red stew, for I am weary.' He was a very hungry young man and he could see nothing but that stew. His conniving brother Jacob saw his opportunity and his brother's weakness and said, 'OK, but first you have to give me your birthright as the eldest son.' This was a big thing in those days and meant that Jacob would now get most of his father's blessing—and also most of his inheritance too. Nevertheless, the 'must-have' mentality was in top gear now and can be seen in

Esau's reply to Jacob: 'Look, I am about to die; so what is this birthright to me?' Esau had an amazing blessing waiting for him in the future, but all he was interested in was having what he wanted and having it right now. So he sold his birthright for a bowl of stew.

You may wonder what the significance of this was. Well, Esau did lose his birthright and Jacob did get it instead. Esau and his family faded into insignificance, while Jacob, later renamed Israel, became the father of the Jewish nation and an ancestor of Jesus himself. Esau was left with nothing.

I'm sure you aren't going to give away your birthright for a bowl of stew, but I hope you can see the principle. We need to make sure we don't fall into the same trap with something we really want but can't really afford. Don't fall into the Esau trap!

Now, this isn't going to be easy because, as I have said, our whole culture is telling us to go for it. What help does God give us in these situations? The answer is 'plenty', and it's not all gloom and doom. As always, God understands our weaknesses and gives us instructions and practical help to get around them. Money problems are no exception.

Firstly, we need to understand what it is that we are feeling when we want something a lot. There is nothing wrong with wanting something badly. The problems start when we want something too badly. God makes it very clear that if anything in our lives is more precious to us than Himself, it is idolatry and a sin. It's there in the first and second of the Ten Commandments, right at the top of the list:

> *You shall have no other gods before Me. You shall not make for yourself an idol in the form of anything in heaven above or on the earth beneath or in the waters below.*
>
> *(Exodus 20:3–4)*

Here comes the sanity check: How can wanting a new car, a bigger house or a PS4 be idolatry? Isn't idolatry about bowing down to false wooden gods and the like? That was certainly true for God's people, the Jews, in the Old Testament, but it's not the thing itself that's important but the state of heart. When people in Israel decided to worship idols they were saying in their hearts, 'I want this to be at the centre of my life; this is what consumes me, what I really want in life.' In other words, God was pushed off of the throne of their lives and something else took His place. You may laugh at the thought of someone preferring to worship a block of wood rather than the living God—but if you want something so badly that it gets in the way of your relationship with God and even takes His place as Number One in your life, you are doing exactly the same thing. Idols come in many forms and can be quite subtle!

Does this description fit you? If so, you are suffering from a dose of idolatry. You might even find that you have a dose of coveting too. 'Coveting' is a word that isn't used much in everyday language these days. It simply means being jealous of somebody who has something you want. Idolatry and covetousness often gang up together on us.

The solution

Now we know what the problem is, but what do we do about it? The simple answer is: Get our perspective sorted out.

Let's unpack that a little. 'Perspective' here means to see things as they really are, not all twisted and out of proportion. Have you ever seen one of those trick photos where there is a person near the camera and one much further away, and with a bit of positioning the photographer can make it look as if the person far away is standing in the palm of the hand of the person near the camera? This works because the perspective of the photo makes the picture seem out of proportion—and so it is when we want something so much that idolatry and covetousness get hold of us and make things look all wrong. We end up wanting something and thinking about it all the time. Often we start noticing other people with the thing we want so that we can't think straight—our perspective goes and suddenly everything is out of proportion. What we want seems so big that it fills our mind so that we think *we must have it*—no matter what the cost. When we are in this frame of mind we can usually invent reasons why we should have what we desire to convince ourselves that we should have it. Once again the advertisers play on this with straplines such as 'because you're worth it'.

'Couldn't happen to me—I'm far too savvy to fall into that trap,' you may be thinking. Well, it could, because if it happened to Adam and Eve when they were still sinless, then it can definitely happen to poor sinners like you and me living in a fallen world.

Adam and Eve had it made in the Garden of Eden. The work was light and actually pleasant to do. All the animals loved them and weren't afraid of them; it was not too hot or too cold; there were no such things as weeds, illness, death, sadness or pain. On top of all that, they had a face-to-face relationship with their loving Creator God. He even walked with them in the garden in the cool of the evening. They wanted for nothing. Except, actually, they did have a want, and that was the trouble. You know the story. They had it all, and the only thing they were not allowed to do was eat the fruit of one tree. Along came the devil in the guise of a serpent and tempted them to *want* the fruit from that very tree. They weren't hungry—they had amazing fruit trees all around them to eat from at any time; but they wanted *that* fruit, fruit from the only tree that was forbidden them. And so their perspective went out the window. Genesis 3:6 says,

> *So when the woman saw that the tree was good for food, that it was pleasant to the eyes, and a tree desirable to make one wise ...*

Notice the key phrases here: was *good for food* (so were the rest, but it was this one they wanted); *pleasant to the eyes* (so were the others, but they had eyes only for this tree now); *desirable* (so were all the others). Their perspective was well and truly gone, so they took the fruit and ate it. In doing so they paid a terrible price and took on a terrible debt they could never repay. They had sinned, and so God, who takes sin and debt very seriously, had no alternative but to keep His promise. They died spiritually on the spot, and death and destruction entered the whole of creation. Death, sickness, sadness and pain became the new norm, and we are still living with these consequences today. So great was that debt that only by God sending His Son, Jesus, to die on the cross to pay for the sin we have all inherited from Adam and Eve can we be redeemed—bought back at a great price—from God's wrath.

When we get ourselves into a situation where our perspective has gone out the window as Adam and Eve's did, we need to get it sorted out. How? By refocusing on the Lord Jesus. This isn't too difficult or complicated; it simply involves spending time with Him—praying and reading His Word. When we do this, things usually sort themselves out.

I think this is what the psalmist is getting at in Psalm 119:36–37:

Incline my heart to Your testimonies,
And not to covetousness.
Turn away my eyes from looking at worthless things,
And revive me in Your way.

As we look at Jesus—His life, His love for us, His death in our place to take our sins away—we will find that the thing we wanted will become just that: a thing, something not really important, and certainly not worth getting all screwed up about. If you suspect that your perspective is off, don't wait, and don't start telling yourself it's OK. Do something about it now. Go straight to Jesus and ask for His forgiveness and to help you get your perspective back—and He will!

Debt: what the Bible says

Now let's have a look at what the Bible says about debt and how seriously God takes it.

A study of the Bible shows up an interesting fact: the word 'lend' occurs twelve times, 'borrow' four times, but 'owe' only seven times.[1] This presents us with a bit of a problem. For example, Romans 13:8 says,

> Owe *no one anything except to love one another, for he who loves another has fulfilled the law [emphasis mine].*

On the other hand, there are verses like Exodus 22:25:

---

1 Based on the New International Version (this might vary from version to version).

> *If you* lend *money to any of My people who are poor among you, you shall not be like a moneylender to him; you shall not charge him interest [emphasis mine].*

The verse in Exodus implies that some of God's people (the poor) will owe money because they have been lent it by others; but the verse in Romans says that God's people should not owe anything to anyone except love. Is this a contradiction? No, of course not; God's Word never contradicts itself. God doesn't make mistakes and this is His inspired Word. So what does it mean? What is it telling us? To find out, we need to dig a little deeper into the passages the verses are taken from and the context they are given in.

The Romans verse is given in the context of a number of other things that are owed. Up to verse 8 the chapter is about our submitting ourselves to ruling authorities or *giving the respect we owe authority* through obedience. In verse 6 this is shown to include paying taxes, which are *owed*. This is expanded in verse 7, and then in verse 8 it is finished off with the words 'Owe no one anything' (or 'Let no debt remain outstanding', NIV). All the things that have been mentioned are things we owe in an ongoing way. These debts are open-ended things that we continue to pay. We should try to pay off all that we owe with the exception of love, because that debt can never be paid. An example of this is our debt to our parents or spouse. We have a constant debt of love and gratitude to them which we continue to pay on a daily basis but can never truly finish paying off. In other words, what verse 8 is telling us is that we should try not to remain in debt to anyone, but, as with love and respect, any debt is to be paid off as best we can.

This then helps us to understand the second passage, Exodus 22:25. Obviously, if the person being talked about in this verse is lending, there must be someone who is borrowing. The Bible here is recognizing that there are times when we need to borrow. This may be borrowing something as simple as a book, a phone or even money. The rule to remember is that any borrowing is a serious commitment. When we borrow, we are making a promise that we will look after whatever it is that is being borrowed and will return it in good condition and as quickly as possible. Borrowing is never to be undertaken lightly. Conversely, lending is never to be undertaken lightly either.

Who to borrow from

Exodus 22:25 suggests that moneylenders did not have a very good reputation back in the time of Moses. Today we have laws to help protect us from the worst excesses of people who lend money but expect it back with a lot of interest. These people are often called 'loan sharks'. They exploit those who want money, giving it to them but with massive interest rates. Such people take advantage of the poor and weak, especially when they are in times of trouble, offering to get them out of financial trouble with a loan but often not telling them how much will have to be paid back. The poor borrower is then left in a downward spiral of trying to pay off this debt but being unable to do so. For example, a mother of four once borrowed £500 to pay off a debt. Seven years later she had paid back £88,000.

If the borrower cannot pay, he or she may even be harassed and threatened. Such 'loan sharks' are evil and you should never consider taking a loan from them. They are breaking the law, because in the UK (and most other Western countries) moneylenders have to be registered and must abide by rules which stop them misleading and threatening people. So if you must borrow money from a person or organization, ensure that they are registered moneylenders. In the UK, the Consumer Credit Public Register lists everyone with a licence as well as everyone who has applied for one or has had one taken away or suspended. It includes all the banks and building societies too. Check this out. If a person or organization is not on it, avoid it.

That's not the end of the story, though. In some countries there is a maximum legal interest rate. In the UK there is not, although there is growing pressure to put this right. Remember that, however loan companies or shopkeepers dress it up, they are out to make money from you. If a deal seems too good to be true, it probably is. There is an old saying in English law: 'Buyer beware!' It is the principle that you are responsible for the item you are buying. When it comes to loans or hire purchase, it means you are responsible for making sure you don't get taken in and that you get the best deal possible. In the next, much longer chapter we'll look in practical detail at how you can do this.

How to get the best deal possible

Here are a few rules to help you find the best deal for your circumstances when getting a loan or buying on hire purchase.

Rule 1: Find out the rate of interest being charged

When you buy things, you probably shop around for the best deal. The same should be true with getting a loan or buying on credit or hire purchase (hire purchase means you buy now and pay later with interest). The shop may offer a deal, but check it out as it may not be the best deal. Shops sometimes get a payment from the loan company for each deal they make, so it is in their interest to sell you their deal—but it may not be in your interest. That is what you should be interested in when looking for a loan or credit deal—*interest*.

What is interest? Interest is the amount you have to pay the loan company, bank or building society for borrowing the money to buy what you want. In the UK it is called the Annual Percentage Rate (APR). APR is simple and easy to understand and compare. On a *credit card* it is charged monthly, so if you take the APR and divide it by twelve (months of the year), then multiply that percentage by the amount owed at the beginning of the month, you have your monthly payment. Here is an example:

> What is the interest on a credit card loan of £1,000 if the APR is 12%?
>
> APR = 12%, amount owed = £1,000
>
> Divide 12 (APR) by 12 (months of year) = 1
>
> Now multiply 1,000 by 1% = 10
>
> So the credit card payment for that month is £10 in interest.

On a *loan* the APR is a little different: it includes all the arrangement fees and other hidden costs, which is good as that means there should be no nasty surprises. It is calculated yearly. For example:

Let's take our £1,000 loan again, paid over 5 years.

APR = 10%, amount owed = £1,000

So in Year 1 of the loan you pay 10% of 1,000 = 100

This is usually paid monthly, so 100 divided by 12 = £8.33 interest per month.

BUT you must also pay off the capital of the loan; this will be:

£1,000 divided by 5 (as it is over 5 years) = £200, or £16.66 per month

At the beginning of Year 2 you have therefore already paid off £200 of the capital, so you only pay interest on £1,000 minus £200, which is £800.

So Year 2's interest is lower—10% of £800, which is £80, or £6.66 per month.

In Year 3 the interest payment will be lower again, and so on.

Because people (and banks) want to be able to budget easily, they prefer the monthly payments always to be the same—not changing every month or year as shown above. So to keep the monthly cost the same your payments will start by paying more of the interest and less capital, and then later in the loan period will pay less interest and more of the capital. As far as you are concerned, though, it all happens automatically and seamlessly. You just pay the same fixed amount throughout.

It is important that you know the APR of any loan you are looking for, not some other measure, such as flat rate (which is often quoted). A flat rate (sometimes called a flat fee) may look better than APR, but because of the way it is calculated it is often more expensive. For instance, a flat rate of 1% per month sounds low, but over a year it will cost you over 21% (APR). Companies sometimes advertise 'Effective APR', known as EAR, but with this it can be more complex to work out exactly what you have to pay back. (It sounds confusing, but this is why you have to be so careful when borrowing money!)

In recent years, particularly during the recession, there has been a huge growth in the number of short-term loan companies. These have sprouted up mainly because during hard times people can't make it from one pay day to the next—an unexpected bill often arrives. Faced with a shortfall for a week or two, people go to these lenders for a relatively small loan of a few hundred pounds which they hope to repay on the next pay day. There are two problems with such loans. Firstly, the APR on them is huge, usually hundreds or even thousands of per cent. Since the loans are short term and the sums involved are usually fairly small, this doesn't look like a huge problem.

Here's an example from a real web-based loan company: Borrowing just £200 for 14 days costs a total of £234.27 with fees—but that is a whopping 5852% APR! This brings us to the second big problem. People who go for such loans are usually 'on the edge' financially, and what happens all too often is that repayment day arrives and they are short of cash again—so they take out another loan to cover the first loan, but this time it's a bit bigger. Before they know it, the debt gets out of control and they end up owing sizeable amounts at huge interest rates. It's a slippery slope. Such loans should be avoided at all costs (excuse the pun). The Internet is full of horror stories about such pay-day loan companies and the cash-strapped people who have fallen foul of them. The UK government announced in January 2105 that they will cap the amount of interest that these short-term loan companies can charge, which is good news; nevertheless, they remain a dangerous way of managing your finances.

Rule 2:
Find out the monthly repayments and the repayment timescale

Usually a loan company, bank or building society will tell you how much the monthly repayments will be. Normally these payments are calculated so as to stay the same over the whole length of the loan in order to help you budget, but do check that this is the case. Of course, a loan taken out over a longer period will cost less to repay per month and the APR will probably be lower, so spreading the loan out over a longer period is fine to help you budget, but you will almost certainly end up paying back a lot more in total because you are paying for longer. Try to find a repayment timescale that you can fairly comfortably afford, because the APR may change and go up or down during the lifetime of the loan. If it does go up, you will find your monthly payments increasing as well! Build in a little slack just in case this happens. This is something else to consider when taking out the loan: Is it a fixed or variable APR loan? If it is fixed, you know there won't be any changes throughout the repayment period. If it is variable, it might go down—but it might also go up.

Rule 3:
Work out what you can afford to repay

This might sound obvious, but people (particularly young people, who are less experienced in handling money) often wildly overestimate what they can afford to repay. The first thing to consider is what your income is. If you don't have a regular and stable monthly income, forget it! Some people have incomes that go up and down a lot. If this is the case for you, a loan is a bad idea—it is nearly impossible to know if you will have enough to meet the monthly repayments. If you don't have an income, or if it is erratic, the loan companies, banks or building societies should refuse you anyway, but recent history is strewn with examples of people getting loans they should never have been allowed to have. Often these people end up bankrupt, and bankruptcy can affect you for the rest of your life, making it difficult or even impossible for you to borrow or even get a mortgage.

If you do have a regular income, write down your monthly incomes on one side of a piece of paper (or use a spreadsheet). On the other side, list all your monthly outgoings. This may need thinking about a bit and you may need to check out old bills. You will need to include things such as spending on clothes, transport, holidays, food, the mortgage or rent, and of course any other loans you may have, including repayment of student loans. Don't forget buying presents for birthdays and Christmas. It might be a good idea to ask someone you trust to check your list. This leads to the next rule.

Rule 4:
Get your advice on the loan from someone you trust

Two heads are better than one in this situation, and a close and trusted friend or relative can be a useful sanity check to ensure you have thought everything through. This is doubly important if you are young and new to the world of loans and borrowing. If you are under eighteen you won't be able to get a loan anyway—but just because you reach the age of eighteen and legally become an adult doesn't mean you should ignore the lifetime of expertise of someone older and hopefully wiser. In this situation, consider getting your parents' advice, especially if they are Christians. Your parents will have had experience in this area, so tap into that. Their first instinct may be to say 'no' straight off (parents are sometimes overprotective—it's in the job description!), but explain what you want the loan for and show that you have done your homework in thinking it through. If after this they still say it's a bad idea, then it probably is. They may be able to suggest alternatives, but if not you would need to be *very* sure you were right before going against their advice.

If you are older, or asking parents is not a viable option, confide in a close friend, one you know and trust and who can be relied on for good sense.

Rule 5: If you start having trouble repaying a loan, seek help

If something does go wrong when you have a loan and you can't keep up the repayments, *seek help and seek it quickly*. Tell the loan company, bank or building society you have borrowed from. They will usually be far more helpful and accommodating if you come to them before the problem gets too serious. They may suggest a longer repayment time or some other help. If this doesn't work, get in touch with the Citizens Advice Bureau. Their advice is free and they have lots of experience in helping people with similar problems. You will find other sources of help listed at the end of this booklet. Make no mistake, though: it will be tough and embarrassing to get out of this hole, and it may take years. Mortgages and some loans are given on the security of your home. This means that if you cannot make the payments, the loan company, bank or building society has the right to repossess your home and sell it to repay the debt. This is a last resort, but in 2012, 33,900 homes were repossessed in the UK. Needless to say, avoid getting into this position if at all possible. I repeat: *if you are getting into difficulties, seek help as soon as possible.*

It is also worth remembering that if you do get into such difficulties, you will find it far more difficult to borrow money in the future. Lenders keep track of borrowers using something called a credit score or credit rating. If your credit rating takes a hit because of bad debt, other lenders will tend not to lend to you. This can be difficult to recover from.

This has got pretty heavy, and hopefully you will never get into such difficulties. There are, however, still a few areas that need exploring. These are the tools that most people use to help them handle their money.

Bank or building society accounts

These are the usual sorts of accounts where you have a chequebook and perhaps a debit card.

Cheques are going out of fashion fast but they will still be with us for a few years yet, and if you are sixteen or over you can have an account with cheques. The cheques you write out are basically a promise that you will pay a sum of money (whatever amount is on the cheque) to the person you make it out to. This person then takes the cheque to a bank or building society and your account gets debited by that amount (that amount is taken out of your account). There is absolutely nothing wrong with having a chequebook, but like everything else it must be handled with care and prayer.

It is possible to write cheques for amounts greater than you have in your account, but this is seriously not advisable. Several things could happen. The bank or building society may 'bounce' the cheque. This means that it doesn't get paid, so the person you gave it to is going to be pretty mad with you and you will have to find another way to pay him or her. The bank may also return the bounced cheque to you with a nasty little letter which will also tell you that they will charge you for bouncing it. This charge can vary a lot but is usually about £30 per cheque. Alternatively, they may pay the cheque but charge you an 'unarranged overdraft fee', which is also expensive.

If you need to use more money than you have in your account you can arrange for an overdraft. This allows you to take out more from your account than you have in it, up to an arranged maximum. This is sometimes called 'going into the red' because years ago the bank would send you statements telling you what you had in your account and any overdraft would be shown in red ink, just to rub it in. Again, this is something to be avoided if possible, but few of us have managed to get through life without having an overdraft at some point. Having an overdraft may be a reasonable thing to do, but it should be looked into on the same basis as a loan because that is basically what it is, and you will certainly be charged for the privilege. It is certainly not 'free money'—there is no such thing. However, if you are a student at college or university you will probably be eligible for a free overdraft. This is not free money—you will have to pay it back when you get a job after studying—but there is no interest charged on it, so you will only pay back exactly what you borrowed. This is a lifeline for students as government loans are usually not enough to live on. If you are thinking of studying and are over eighteen, have a word with your bank or building society about this and see what they have to offer. Many offer other freebies, such as reduced-cost railcards, so it may pay to shop around for the best deal. (See Chapter 4 for further advice for students.)

The other thing you often get with a bank or building society account is a debit card. A debit card is a really useful electronic card with a small computer chip in it. It has a code number on it which can be used for making purchases remotely (e.g. over the Internet) as well as a PIN (Personal Identification Number) which allows you to use it for purchases in shops and so on. All you do is insert the card in a reader, tap in the PIN and the purchase is completed. It can also be used in an ATM (Automatic Teller Machine) to withdraw cash from your account. Note that not all ATMs are free to use: some make a charge for each withdrawal you make. The ATM must say on it somewhere either how much it will charge or if it is free to use. The fee is usually not very much (about £2), but it is worth keeping in mind if there is a free alternative nearby.

As long as you remember the PIN and never write it down, a debit card is very safe. Make sure the PIN (usually only four digits) is not something that others might guess if they stole your card but is memorable enough so that you won't ever forget it. When tapping in the PIN in a shop or in an ATM, make sure that no one else can see what you are tapping in. A thief might try to see the number and then steal the card. If you do lose it or have it stolen, report it to your bank or building society straight away. They will block the card so that it can't be used in an ATM or in a shop. Speedy reporting is important because if a thief does access your account, he or she could drain it dry in minutes.

A subtle danger in having and using a debit card is that it makes spending seem a bit unreal. No money changes hands and all you do is tap in a number and it's all done. This can make spending a little too easy, but it is difficult to go beyond the money you have in your account. Usually the purchase simply won't go through if you don't have the funds—which can be embarrassing, but at least it won't cost you anything.

The debit card is now a basic tool found in most people's wallets or purses; almost everyone has one as it is very useful and is an alternative to carrying cash, which can sometimes be risky. As long as you can keep tabs on what you have left in your account as you use it, there should be little problem using it sensibly—and keeping tabs on your account is extremely easy today using monthly balance sheets from your bank, short account slips available from most ATMs or Internet banking.

Credit cards

Credit cards are quite different from debit cards because they do not depend on what you have in your account. When you buy something using a credit card, you are really using the bank or building society's money—you are borrowing from them. Usually there is an upper limit for what you can spend, but this can be quite high, and often the banks and building societies will increase your limit if you tend to spend up to the limit regularly.

Credit cards are very useful, but they are also really dangerous at the same time. The negative side is that you can spend lots of money that feels as if it's yours, but which is still actually a loan, and the bank or building society will charge you interest (usually quite a lot) on the loan just as if it were cash you were borrowing. People can have more than one credit card and can easily run up thousands of pounds of debt in a short time. At the time of writing, people in the UK owe a staggering £64.7 billion on credit cards—that's just over £1,000 for every person in the country! On average, every adult in the UK has two credit cards—that's about 58 million cards in total. Usually you pay a monthly fee to the bank or building society that at least covers the interest that needs to be paid but doesn't reduce the amount you actually owe. If you miss a payment, you normally have to pay an extra fee—so it all adds up so that the banks and building societies make a profit of about £6 billion each year. And it is often young, inexperienced people who get themselves into trouble most easily.

Yet, on the other hand, credit cards are incredibly useful. Like a debit card, a credit card is also an alternative to carrying cash around with you. If it is used carefully and responsibly, a credit card is a really useful tool. There are two main advantages of a credit card. Firstly, consumer protection: if the company you buy from goes bust or the item you ordered on the Internet is faulty or doesn't turn up, and if the cost is between £10 and £60,260 (these figures may change over time), you can get your money back. The same applies if your card is used fraudulently. Secondly, many credit cards offer incentives such as cashback, air miles or loyalty points. These incentives are small, but every little helps.

Here are some rules to help you use a credit card wisely.

RULE 1:
DON'T USE STORE CARDS; DO SHOP AROUND

Store cards are credit cards offered by some high-street retailers. It is best to avoid these as the interest rates on them are often a lot higher than those on bank or building society cards, although some supermarket cards are similar. It pays to shop around for the lowest interest rate.

RULE 2:
DON'T PAY INTEREST

If you make an arrangement with your bank or building society to pay off each month's credit card bill you won't have to pay interest. I would highly recommend doing this. I've had a credit card for many years and have never paid a penny in interest on it! This is the way to go: you get all the benefits and none of the hassle, it's paid automatically if you set up a standing order (these are explained below), and you get a statement to check at the end of each month. Of course, you do need to have enough in your bank or building society account to meet the repayments.

RULE 3:
TAKE THE SAME PRECAUTIONS WITH A CREDIT CARD THAT YOU WOULD WITH A DEBIT CARD

See the section earlier for precautions concerning using debit cards.

RULE 4:
STICK TO A SINGLE CREDIT CARD IF POSSIBLE

Make life easy for yourself. The only reason to have more than one credit card is if you intend to juggle your finances between them. This is not a good move as it can get very complex and is a sure-fire way to get into debt. The only exception to this is if you have a credit card to use for your job; if that's the case, you can be sure that your employer will be very careful to ensure you use it properly.

There are a couple of other things you need to know about bank and building society accounts. I mention them only briefly as they are simply aids to you getting the best out of your account and managing your finances.

Standing orders (often simply called SOs)

Standing orders are agreements you set up with your bank or building society to make regular payments, usually monthly. You simply give the bank or building society the details of who to pay and when, and they will do the rest. Standing orders are usually used to pay either for money that has been lent to you or for bills that are spread out over a long period, such as utility bills (gas, electricity, etc.). They're neat because they remove the hassle of having to remember to pay for something every month. The other benefits are that you have total control over them and they are free. You can stop one or change it at any time. The only downside is that you will need to make sure that there is enough money in your account when it's time for the SO to be paid. If not, the bank or building society may pay it and charge you for going into the red—or not pay it at all and still charge you!

Direct debits

Direct debits work in a similar way to standing orders but with a few important differences. When you set up a standing order you are in control of the payments. When a direct debit is set up it's those you are paying who have the control. It is they who decide how much you pay back each month, and they have the power to change that amount. This sounds alarming at first, but direct debits are very popular and a lender has to let you know in writing if they intend to change the repayments, so you do have fair warning. You can then have the direct debit stopped—but this should be done only as a last resort, as it won't impress the bank or the person/company you owe money to! Direct debits can be very good for bills that might vary in amount from time to time, and often the lender will give a small discount on your payments because they like the flexibility of being able to change them. So the key thing with direct debits is to check what you are paying regularly, monitor any changes in payment and make sure you have enough in your account to cover the payment. If you stay watchful, they are perfectly safe.

Something especially for students

OK, so I've made it clear that debt is to be avoided whenever possible and have helped you to understand the good and bad points of most of the things you need to know about out there in the money world. Sometimes, though, it seems that even careful people can't avoid going into debt—big debt! What do I mean?

Well, in England, Wales and Northern Ireland, if you intend to go to university to study, then unless you have really rich (and generous) parents you are going to find yourself having to pay through the nose for the privilege.

University top-up fees and student loans (in England, Wales and Northern Ireland)

Going to university has always been a time when young people find it hard to survive financially, but when I was at university there were no top-up fees for courses and the government actually gave students a grant (money given that you didn't need to pay back). This meant that, although it was very hard, I was able to come out of my time at university with a degree and no debt. But that's all history now, because top-up fees alone are thousands of pounds a year and the government usually won't give you any help except in the form of a student loan, although some loan-free grants and bursaries may be available for the most cash-strapped.

The government will lend you money to pay for the top-up fees the universities charge (Wales has lower top-up fees than England and Northern Ireland; Scotland currently has no top-up fees) and also a maintenance loan to help you pay the bills, but they want it paid back, and with interest! It's not all bad: the loans don't have to start being paid back until you are in a job and earning £21,000 per year, and the interest rate you pay is pretty low (at the moment at least). An average young person completing a three-year degree can expect to end up owing an average of about £44,000 (2014 figures). That's a lot of dosh! Finding accurate figures of how long it will take to pay off the student loan is difficult and depends on how much you will earn, but following a three-year course many students are likely to still be paying off the debt in their fifties! One morsel of comfort is that anything left unpaid after thirty years is written off. In the time it has taken me to write this booklet, several schemes to improve the student loan system in England, Wales and Northern Ireland have been considered and scrapped. One thing is certain: the problem isn't going to go away, and some people have claimed that it is a 'ticking time bomb' for people's finances. Certainly it is already making it harder for young people to get mortgages.

How much you pay back depends on what you earn. If you earn less than £21,000 you pay nothing. Above that, you will pay back 9% of what you earn above £21,000. For example, If you earn £25,000 you will repay £30 per month, and if you earn £30,000 you will repay £67 per month.

Regardless of the politics concerned, I think it is very sad that young people should be stuck with such a debt—but that's the reality of the situation, so we have to deal with it.

There is a choice, of course. You don't have to go to university and get a degree, and it's worth considering whether university is right for you. The figures, though, do suggest that it is still worth it for most people most of the time. In the UK you are likely to earn about 25% more with a degree than with just A levels—that equates to about £160,000 over a working lifetime. You will probably get a better paid job with a degree, but it will take a long time before it pays for itself.

However, it's about far more than the arithmetic of what you will earn. You need to know that it's God's will for you to go to university. For this you will need to seek Him in prayer, in the reading of His Word, in the wisdom of your parents (especially if they are Christians) and in the wisdom of people you respect spiritually, such as your youth leaders, elders or pastor.

Student loans in Scotland

If you have lived in Scotland for three years or more the situation is different. In Scotland there is the graduate endowment scheme. The Students Award Agency for Scotland (SAAS) pays Scottish students fees for their study in Scotland and the rest of the UK. This is a great help in keeping the level of debt down.

Help for students

If you do believe that it's right for you to go to university, what can you do to ease this debt? The most likely help will probably come in the form of a bursary.

Bursaries

Many universities have given bursaries (money to help you study, usually with few strings attached) for many years, but now the government (in England, Wales and Northern Ireland) have told them to give some of the student top-up fees back as extra bursaries. Some universities make these well known so that they are easy to find and access; others don't. It is well worth checking a university's website or contacting its student support services. These bursaries can be for several thousand pounds—a real help—and may influence you in your choice of university. Additionally, the government has directed universities and colleges to institute hardship funds. These are aimed at very specific needs such as those of students with children or those leaving care, but might still be useful. More information can be found at https://www.gov.uk/

extra-money-pay-university/university-and-college-hardship-funds.

There may also be trust funds and sponsorships available for students from lower-income families. Some bursaries are means-tested; others are not. Some bursaries are conditional upon getting good A level, or A level equivalent, grades before taking up the university place.

Conclusion

Handling money and avoiding debt needs common sense, planning and, above all, God's guidance. Armed with these things you should be able to avoid the many pitfalls that exist and which ensnare so many people. Borrowing money or getting something with a loan is a serious matter but should not be too much of a problem if you are careful and keep your wits about you.

Remember that many of the problems associated with money are the consequences of having a wrong heart attitude, one which is not God-honouring and is basically selfish. The Bible tells us in 1 Timothy 6:10 that the love of money (not money itself) is the root of all kinds of evil. Christians are not immune from getting into money trouble, but we have a Bible that gives us much guidance in this area—not just about money and borrowing, but, more importantly, about sin, sinful desires and human nature. With God's Spirit in your heart, an open Bible in your hand and an attitude of prayer, you won't go far wrong.

Where can I get further help?

I am aware that most of the resources listed here are Internet-based and that if you are in financial difficulty you may not have access to the Internet. If that is the case, go to your local library. Nearly all council-run libraries offer free Internet access (you may have to book a time slot).

A word of warning: Some websites mimic real help websites but are actually run by commercial companies that are out to make money from people in financial difficulty. Any websites I have listed here are safe, and there are many other sites that are genuine—but beware: some are not. If you choose to look elsewhere, avoid at all costs any site that asks you for money.

Your church

I am assuming that if you are a Christian, you regularly attend a church (if you don't, you should).

Many forward-thinking churches have support in place for members in any difficulty, including those with money problems. You should be able to get confidential advice and help by contacting whoever is in charge of this or your pastor, elders or deacons.

Christians Against Poverty (CAP)

This is a very useful organization if you get into debt problems or if you just want to learn more so as to avoid debt. Christians Against Poverty is a charity that gives free help to anyone in debt. They provide help in three main ways. Firstly, they run local help centres. By entering your postcode on their website (see below) you can find your local debt centre and can arrange an appointment where Christians will help and advise you on how to sort things out. Secondly, they run a CAP Money Course, usually in association with local churches. This course is designed to help you avoid getting into trouble in the first place by equipping you to take control of your finances so that you can budget, save and spend wisely. There are also other types of course available, including CAP Money Students, CAP Money Youth and CAP Money Ministers. One of my sons who worked with CAP material while at university recommends the student course as a great help for all students wondering how to survive financially at university. Thirdly, they run CAP Job Clubs for those out of work and seeking employment.

All these services are free and are run by Christians. Visit their website: https://capuk.org/.

Debt Advisory Centre

This service offers help to those who already have debt problems. It is not available for everyone—by completing a simple questionnaire on the website you can see if you qualify. Visit www.debtadvisorycentre.co.uk.

Citizens Advice Bureau

CAB have many years of experience in helping people both avoid money troubles and get out of them. They offer lots of online help as well as local offices you can visit. Advice varies depending on where you live in the UK, so when you visit their website, www.citizensadvice.org.uk, you will need to select your location. Recent changes in the funding of CAB have led to a reduction in the specific help they offer for those with money troubles, but they remain a useful resource.

National Debtline

This is a government-funded phone line (0808 808 4000) and website, www.nationaldebtline.org, where you can get free impartial and confidential advice if you have debt problems.

And finally ...

HM Revenue & Customs offer a list of organizations you can get help from through the Money Advice Service at https://www.moneyadviceservice.org.uk/en/tools/debt-advice-locator.

Booklets in the *Help!* series include …

HELP! How Can I Ever Forgive? (PAUL WILLIAMS)
ISBN 978-1-84625-527-4

HELP! I Can't Forgive (JIM NEWCOMER)
ISBN 978-1-84625-325-6

HELP! I Can't Handle All These Trials (JOEL JAMES)
ISBN 978-1-84625-324-9

HELP! I Can't Submit to My Husband (GLENDA HOTTON)
ISBN 978-1-84625-321-8

HELP! I Feel Ashamed (SUE NICEWANDER)
ISBN 978-1-84625-320-1

HELP! I Have Breast Cancer (BRENDA FRIELDS)
ISBN 978-1-84625-216-7

HELP! I'm Living with Terminal Illness (REGGIE WEEMS)
ISBN 978-1-84625-319-5

HELP! I've Been Deployed (RODDY MACLEOD)
ISBN 978-1-84625-459-8

HELP! I've Been Diagnosed with Multiple Sclerosis (JO JOHNSON)
ISBN 978-1-84625-525-0

HELP! My Baby Has Died (REGGIE WEEMS)
ISBN 978-1-84625-215-0

HELP! My Toddler Rules the House (PAUL AND KAREN TAUTGES)
ISBN 978-1-84625-221-1

HELP! She's Struggling with Pornography (RACHEL COYLE)
ISBN 978-1-84625-246-4

HELP! Someone I Love Has Alzheimer's (DEBORAH HOWARD)
ISBN 978-1-84625-323-2

HELP! Someone I Love Has Been Abused (JIM NEWHEISER)
ISBN 978-1-84625-222-8

HELP! Someone I Love Has Cancer (DEBORAH HOWARD)
ISBN 978-1-84625-217-4

HELP! Someone I Love Has Dementia (JO JOHNSON)
ISBN 978-1-84625-458-1

HELP! Someone I Love Has Depression (JIM WINTER)
ISBN 978-1-84625-460-4